P9-DGU-947

Dogs
E636.7 Mei   160041

Wilton Public Library

DATE DUE			
WPC			

Wilton Public Library
1215 Cypress Street
P.O. Box 447
Wilton, IA 52778

My First Pet

Dogs

Wilton Public Library
1215 Cypress Street
P.O. Box 447
Wilton, IA 52778

by Cari Meister

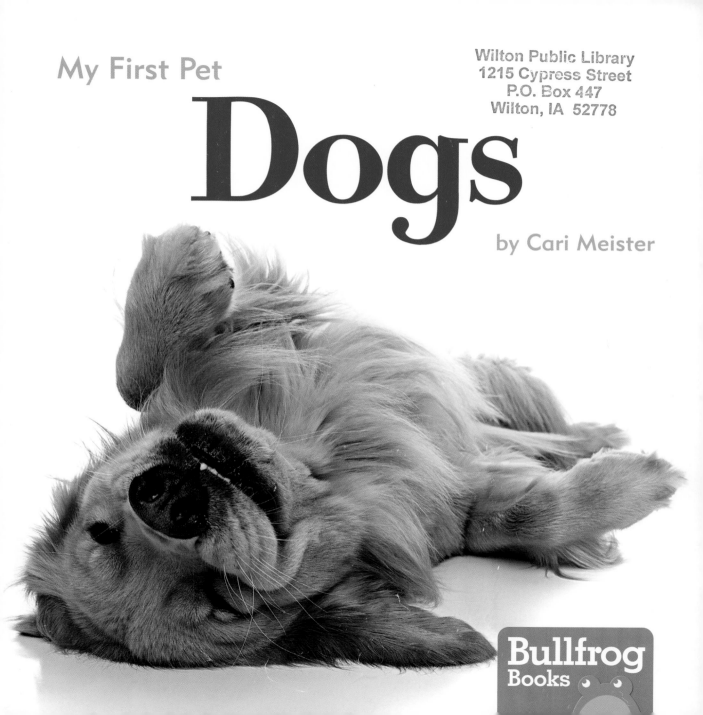

Bullfrog
Books

Ideas for Parents and Teachers

Bullfrog Books let children practice reading informational text at the earliest reading levels. Repetition, familiar words, and photo labels support early readers.

Before Reading
- Ask the child to think about pet dogs. Ask: What do you know about dogs?
- Look at the picture glossary together. Read and discuss the words.

Read the Book
- "Walk" through the book and look at the photos. Let the child ask questions. Point out the photo labels.
- Read the book to the child, or have him or her read independently.

After Reading
- Prompt the child to think more. Ask: What do you need to take care of a dog or puppy? Would you like to own a dog?

Bullfrog Books are published by Jump!
5357 Penn Avenue South
Minneapolis, MN 55419
www.jumplibrary.com

Copyright © 2015 Jump! International copyright reserved in all countries. No part of this book may be reproduced in any form without written permission from the publisher.

Library of Congress Cataloging-in-Publication Data

Meister, Cari, author.
  Dogs / by Cari Meister.
     pages cm. — (My first pet)
  Summary: "This photo-illustrated book for early readers tells how to take care of a pet dog" — Provided by publisher.
  Audience: 005-008.
  Audience: K to grade 3.
  Includes bibliographical references and index.
  ISBN 978-1-62031-122-6 (hardcover) —
  ISBN 978-1-62496-189-2 (ebook) —
  ISBN 978-1-62031-143-1 (paperback)
  1. Dogs — Juvenile literature. I. Title.
  SF426.5.M45 2015
  636.7'0887—dc23
                                        2013042369

Series Editor: Rebecca Glaser
Series Designer: Ellen Huber
Book Designer: Anna Peterson
Photo Researcher: Casie Cook

Photo Credits: All photos by Shutterstock except: Alamy/Arterra Picture Library, 16–17; Dreamstime/ Ngo Thye Aun, 19; Getty Images/Colorblind, 8; Getty Images/LWA, 12–13, 23br; Getty Images/ Thomas Strand, 14–15; Superstock/Blend Images, Spread 20–21; Superstock/Exactostock, 10–11

Printed in the United States of America at Corporate Graphics, in North Mankato, Minnesota.
3-2014
10 9 8 7 6 5 4 3 2 1

Table of Contents

Taking Care of a Dog 4

What Does a Dog Need? 22

Picture Glossary 23

Index 24

To Learn More 24

Taking Care of a Dog

Sid wants a dog.

How do you care for a dog?

Dogs need exercise.

Mia plays fetch with Roy.

Dogs need healthy food.

Kai feeds Red two times a day.
If Red is good, he gets treats.

food

treats

9

Dogs need fresh water.
Ava fills Ike's bowl.

11

Dogs need check-ups.
Ed takes Bo to the vet.
The vet gives Bo shots.

vet

13

Dogs need to be kept clean.

Muffin gets a bath.

Dogs need to know
the rules.

Taj takes Mo
to dog school.

Mo learns.

He sits. He stays.

Dogs need a place to sleep.

kennel

Rocko sleeps in his kennel.
He feels safe.

Dogs need love.

Sky hugs Max.

Dogs are great pets!

What Does a Dog Need?

dog toys
Give your dog toys and play with him so he doesn't get bored.

food
Dogs need healthy food every day.

collar
A band that goes around a dog's neck and holds a tag.

water
Dogs need fresh water every day.

leash
You need a leash to walk your dog.

Picture Glossary

fetch
A game where an owner throws an object and the dog goes and gets it and brings it back.

treats
Special foods such as dog biscuits.

kennel
A cage that keeps a dog safe.

vet
An animal doctor.

Index

bath 14

check-ups 12

exercise 6

fetch 6

food 8

kennel 19

love 20

rules 16

school 16

shots 12

treats 9

vet 12

To Learn More

Learning more is as easy as 1, 2, 3.

1) Go to www.factsurfer.com

2) Enter "pet dog" into the search box.

3) Click the "Surf" button to see a list of websites.

With factsurfer.com, finding more information is just a click away.